A GALLERY OF HUSBANDS

Oliver Andrew

A GALLERY OF HUSBANDS contains works of
fiction. Any similarity to actual persons or events is
purely intentional.

ISBN 978-1-907897-03-0

A *NightWriters Editions* book.
NightWriters Editions have been inaugurated in order to focus attention on
individual writers living in or near Brighton whose work merits publication.

NightWriters Editions are published by NightWriters Press
www.nightwriters.org.uk

Acknowledgements

A Gallery of Husbands is a *NightWriters Editions* book. Brighton NightWriters is a not-for-profit organisation furthering the interests of creative writers living in or near Brighton. NightWriters' principal activities are the holding of regular meetings at which writers are able to present their work for constructive criticism, and the publication of members' finished work. Further details can be found on our website.

www.nightwriters.org.uk

The author would like to thank Jonathan Cunningham and Tim Shelton-Jones for their encouragement and hard work, Joe Evans for the cover design, and all those members of Brighton NightWriters who, over the years, have offered such helpful suggestions.

Brief Biography

Oliver Andrew taught in a Brighton Sixth Form College for 27 years. Now retired, he recycles himself as a French mountain peasant in the summer, but returns to Brighton to keep warm in the winter. He's married, with two children and three grand-children.

Contents

A Gallery of Husbands

Mr Cinderella

Come on, admit it, you fancied him too
My trim decisive henchman.
But where is he now? For it was he who
Dreamt up that fiasco plan
      To save us two:

The too-small slipper of rigid glass!
"The Ball!", the power-cut!, "The Competition!"
Half the country's girls with blisters!
How we giggled together ..... But then
      The Hardup sisters.

So now I'm stuck with an ex-tweenie
With size 0 feet and tinkling laughter,
Likes to call herself "your little queenie";
So they all lived happily ever after,
      Eh, Dandini?

Dirty Old Man

Mallards at the iron gate,
Noisy, edgy, censorious, sedate,
Hold loiterers to ransom;
Cyclists cycle, by the river
Little toddlers frisk or shiver,
(Mine are gone, and gone for ever),
I smile at one: she tells her mum
Whose eyes flash blue alarms. Off they go,
Can't be too careful these days, you know.

Two girls, some schoolboys for their fags,
My neighbour, swathed in plastic bags,
I wave, but she can hardly see;
Still, plenty of bustle to look at
And perhaps someone will stop and chat
(I'm a widower, but clean and smart).
A loony, care of the community,
Nine men in football shirts, a jay,
No litter - the park's at its best today.

I savour my skills: birds, Tennyson,
Remembering times long gone ....
Survival on the Normandy beaches ....
Those girls, that one has just *her* look
Of promise only one man would unlock,
Of trust, of sunrise certainty, of luck,
(She has a lovely face. Who'll share my riches?)
Of risk shunned, skirted, shared, then flirted with,
Well over the limit at her death ....

I stare at the familiar trees.
Suddenly, she sees my sympathies,
And thinks I'm watching her,
Leching at too-young girls, my hand
Too occupied, my face too bland;
She says as much to her friend
(Who is this? And what is here?)
They bridle, over-knowledgeable, flawed;
Study the dust then, better be ignored.

The man who married a spinster

Weeks after our wedding I still had to
Fight my way through yards of pink lace frill soused
In lavender-water, and pastel-blue
Nighties with crochet work in the most
Improbably decorous places.

Then, less than a year later, she decided
That too much fuss had been made over it
And hadn't we better wait a bit?
So we began sleeping each in our own bed;
And in separate rooms too before long.

How much of this is my fault, I wonder?
I've done *all* I *can*, and found no means
Not love, not poetry, not pity,
To ravish her indifference;
I've *done* all *I* can, and here we sit
And I am writing this and she is
Knitting tiny garments. For nieces.

In the End

In the end he took a broken chair
And sat smoking up at his allotment,
Watching his cabbages, parsley and pigeons;
She took to nibbling, bits of this, bits of that.
Till once a week her sons borrowed the milk-float
To take her to market. All Old Road
Turned out to watch as they backed up to the door
Then stood on the shafts to hold the pony down
While she fell slowly backwards in,
Her gasping, flubbery, mountainous, grieving swags
Hailed by the yelling babies and the barking dogs.

I've a picture of her as a girl
So slim then and serious.
She wears a high frilled collar with a brooch.
Her hands that never learnt to write
Are kept out of shot,
Her eyes are grey and prim,
But her mouth's agog for knowledge and kisses.
You can see why her young man
(My great-grandfather)
Walked every Saturday night across the Pennines
After work, twenty miles in the dark,
To court her,
And back in time for Monday clocking-on.
Exercise enough, you'd think,
But it was his heart that dried up first.

Mr Sleeping Beauty

Sunlit May, but I was indoors frowsting.
Doggedly, a dream of a winter wood
Was trying to tell me ... what? Its wet nose
Thrust a mossy litter of old coppicing,
Root-riven chalk, brownish and purplish staves,
Into my mind. Who was it looking for?

Something in me sought it out until
I was lost, made me have to go on
And on, hacking through swags of brambles,
Mindsets of centuries, cobwebs and bents,
Then crumbling stonework - suddenly a door.
Inside, creepers and psychotherapies
Had got her head, were pinning her down;
Armed with somniloquence and love
I crashed through like the cavalry, and kissed her.

Well, I expect you've forgotten the rest
Of the story! Now she's taken over,
Power-dressed, she stalks the corridors of sleep,
Buzzing with wit, intelligence and beauty,
Attracting admiration, envy and despair;
I've woken her all right: who'll waken me?

Rocket

You rocket up and
Off, gasping your purple stars
Leaving me earthbound

Mr Scheherazade

I knew before I married her
That creativity has its misuses;
I'm old, I know that she's got someone else,
But I love her excuses.

In Bed

A cool rim of ear
On my palm. I envy her
So vulnerable.

We grew colder

We grew colder, the house and I,
While you were away.

Now you're back, you
       tidy tea towels
       pat a cushion
       pick a thread off my collar
       walk round to re-arrange.

Warm us, re-take possession.

Mr Beeton

With sickening speed it became an obsession:
Never the same meal twice,
I stood for hours behind a trolley
While she analysed a price.

The house was over-run with pot-plants,
She checked them day by day;
And: "Where's my Fair Isle pullover?"
"You needed a new one anyway."

My papers unfindable in pyramids:
"Yes, dear, but they look so nice",
And would I give 'a man's view' of
A sixteenth sort of chocolate slice.

Our home became a Petri dish,
I took an office to work at;
She drove herself to death at 28
(I bet you didn't know that?)

Now I can leave things where I know they'll stay,
I breakfast every day on kippers,
I mourn her unspent energy,
But potter in my favourite slippers.

Reality has outflanked me here: I believe Isabella Beeton, author of The
Book of Household Management, and after whom a century of cookery
books has been named, to be far better known to the general public than her
husband. Hence this poem. But though Samuel gets 13 lines in
Encyclopaedia Britannica, under the history of British publishing, there is
no reference to Isabella by name.

Mr. Olympia (after Manet)

When it was first suggested, she was the keen one:
"You know how I like to look
They'll only be like a mirror."
I had to insist on the soigné hair, the stillness.

If only she'd yawn or stretch,
Smile lazily, blush, or panic,
You could really go for her, couldn't you?
Rumple her hair quick now throw the other
Slipper away ...... Mmmmmmmmmm!

Do the ladies see something else maybe?
It's not what Manet saw -
That flawed unvirginal rose
Clash with the black calm gaze -
Yes, it's a man's picture all right,
Her eyes a hand-off, her hand an "eyes-on",
What is it that the woman wants?

And what do you want?
But for that nakedness
You could advance and kiss her hand,
Present your roses or Leonidas,
Observe the conventional decorum,
Murmur: "Mes hommages, Madame"
But as it is, you're men unmanned.

She was half-right only; it wasn't long
Before I came to like it - more indeed -
Saw more reflections there than hers.
You still can't tell what you'd do, can you?
Looking at paintings isn't enough?
Come up and see her in the flesh sometime,
Measure your corruption, know thyself, eh?
I'm offering forbidden fruit.

Infidelities

Caught lying in the double bed
With best friend, or au pair, or three,
Or honey-coloured chambermaid,
    That's clear, we'd all agree.

Probably too about a chap
Imagining in bed, by stealth,
She's darker, blonder, talks less crap,
    Above all, less herself.

And, being married, if we choose
To spend our time and love on pay,
The house, the kids, TV, or booze,
    Would that count, would you say?

Scribbling verses, hiding words,
Slyly waiting till she goes out
(Poems are single-parent bastards)
    Minor cheating, no doubt?

We hardly notice at the start,
Don't want to see the crystal's flaw,
Always claiming it's not like that
    We love her as before.

Looking for warmth, another's wit,
We marry to avoid the chill,
Loneliness, the habit of deceit,
    Then find we need them still.

Fear to face outwards, fear to cleanse
Inner addiction, turn together
Little plots to secret gardens
    Where we flower, but wither.

9

Anniversary

Are we ready then?
Let's go, she says
Slipping her nightie off.
I go out to the car
And wait with the baskets
Knowing she won't be long
Now.

Mr Mona Lisa

A rich man has his wife's portrait done -
It adds that touch of culture to a name.
He was the best, everybody said.
He charged satisfactorily high, and
You could trust your wife at sittings.

At the interview he came across well,
Asked me which way she should face,
What she'd be wearing. He explained
His jargon - silverpoint, minever,
Chiaroscuro, cinnabar, whatever -
And which colour symbolised each element:
Red stood for fire, though copper burns green,
That I do remember; and I could
Understand: "The body is the outward
Expression of the soul which shapes it;
Painters must undo life, peel the soul."
We bankers too must see beneath the skin
The dog, the power-keen indecisive;
That was OK then, so I took him on.

When I wasn't busy, I dropped in;
He fussed about with paints and brushes
Or littered the floor with quick sketches;
A quartet of viols helped her sit
Unscowling, imperturbable.
No expense spared. I winked at her.

Four years he took! When it was complete
I gave a private view - they *did* enthuse,
Admired the "*sfumato* texturing",
The "composition", the "elusiveness",
"Ah!" they said, "she is older than the rocks
Among which she sits, and her hands
Are tinged with the secrets of the grave."
"This is immortal, you lucky man,"
They said, "you're Mona Lisa's husband
For all the world. For ever", they said.

What was all this? Why didn't they see
It was all wrong? - She was 26,
She'd never laid out a corpse; and then
He'd made her fat, with a menacing
Lop-sided smirk and droopy eyelids.
Was this the visible expression
Of her soul? What figure did I cut?

I certainly wasn't going to pay.
He took it with him: without its primers,
Paint, turpentine, bitumen, the sketches
Burned with a hard gem-like flame,
"No *sfumato* there, thank you" we laughed together.

Mrs Donne

Sir, less than kisses do letters mingle souls,
Come home and let us blend them into wholes.
Come live with me and be my love
And we will some new pleasures prove.
To teach thee, I'll be naked first, and then
Why need I have more covering than a man?
License my roving hands, and let them go
Before, behind, around, above, below....
No, bed is fine - but I need TLC,
Forgo all others, say nice things to me.

But on you go, with prohibitions, paradoxes,
Unnecessary new unorthodoxies,
Sermons on young girls you'll never excite,
What if the present were the world's last night?
Stop juggling words and wit, homewards remove,
For God's sake hold your tongue and let me love.

Eve

In Eden, first thing in the morning,
As light sprawled on the grass,
He was up and about, naming.
"Let it be *light*" he said. And it was *light*.
Then, *fish, woman, blood, tree, horse*;
Their names curled off his lips
To master, preserve, manipulate.
I followed him, learning.
"*San? Son*?" I offered. "*Dreep*?"
He frowned. "No". Well, he's the boss.

Bream, wife, crimson, apple, yearling,
On flowed the river of names:
My slippery tongue
Found subtle coils to link them:
Because, more, but, if ....

Early on, chaos crept back at night.
I shook him awake, saying
"A man's gotta do what a man's gotta do"
Red-eyed, he staggered out, mumbling
Pluck, duck, fuck, suck,
Tall, tail, teal, till,
Heap, sheep, leap, creep, peep, sleep ....

Gradually
He dominated.
The river looped to a sluggish thread.

Then it was finished.

We learnt *knowledge, sin,* and *death.*
But at least we're out of there.
Now we've children, he's a proper job;
He can say *weep, toil, blame,*
But also *Eve*
And *love.*

Mr Griselda

Oh don't just sit there, meek and patient,
If you really loved me, you would be
Busy finding ways of pleasing me.

> It must remain forever pristine:
> A tinkling beck among the sombre fells
> Sheds will and purity as it falls.

What fools and peasants get, a love
Decelerating to affection.
Is not enough - I want perfection.

> It must have single-mindedness:
> A candid torrent's only purpose is
> Obedience to gravity's.

So love me more than I love myself:
Give up your job, your friends, your cat,
Children - oh especially that.

> It must be endlessly unselfish:
> I'm standing by a lake - a pebble thrown
> Just goes kerVLUNKsh..sh..sh..and then is gone.

Don't talk to, look at, even think of
Other men. Strip. Kneel. Open wide.
Would you still love me if I tied

You up? I wonder .. Hm ... One must
Go all the way and you seem ready to,
I test my love by testing you.

14

It must be unconditional:
As blackbirds sing at sunset or
The waves unsubtly stalk the shore.

Why sometimes do I have a dream
Of you just smiling meek-and-patiently
While I throw words against a rising sea?

Going to Bed

I'm quicker in: come on, come on,
But you - check the alarm
              put your shoes neatly
              unclip your ear-rings
              catch my eye
As I lie grinning absolutely still
You unhook things with a tidy wriggle
              are naked
              snuggle in next to me
              "Hello" you say.

Sock

My sock's been out for a week.
It struggles a bit in the wind,
But the blackbirds have got quite used
To its frozen toe twisted round the line.
Over breakfast we look at it,
Wondering why our nearest and dearest
Doesn't go to bring it in.

Moving on

Warm light in the east and time for the first bus,
Dew on the grass, as they do it so easy,
Jacket over one shoulder, whistling off-tune,
Leaving someone for ever, but going to
What matters more for them, which is .... well, what?
How can anything matter more than that
Someone you've given yourself to, and they to you,
Whose ways and body you hold next to your own?
It's just flesh, same as theirs, as they do it so easy,
Swinging a holdall, whistling over the wet grass.

King Anne

"First it was ordained for the procreation of children."
No problem there - she shook with life,
Like flames or tinfoil scattering it,
And we were young.
Duty and our spiralling genes
Cracked us like a whip.
Afterwards we lay like spoons,
Waiting; or I pressed my ear to her,
Listened for life to quicken and kick.
Seventeen babies in as many years. All died.
(You never knew that, did you?)
But on she went, giving it away:
"A lady in diamonds and a long black hood",
She laid her Touch on scrofulous children,
They didn't die.

Without that common purpose,
It was other women who put us asunder.

Affairs of State are discussed in her parlour.
Silence falls as I enter for tea,
Like a centurion clanking in
On a flute sonata. Then
"Why, here's George, dear."
"Hullo George."
"Now, will you be mother, dear?"
"Yes please, dahling." They giggle.
We pass the time of day.
Strained counsel. Cold tea.
"Do you think George would like a pastry, dear?"
"Perhaps he might prefer a muffin?"
Am I a poodle? A block?
Where's the ordained "mutual society,
Help and comfort" in this?

Everyone knows she's dead.
Was I ever alive?

It's OK

It's OK to write about menarche and things of that kind -
Pregnancy, breast-feeding - we certainly don't envy you these -
But you have the timeless rhythms, you learn a map of seas,
The body swelling on the tides and leaving pools behind.

After a month, or half your life, you're back to where you were,
(No such knowledge underpins us, no cycles tend or bend,
Any ache in the prostate may be announcing the end)
The sense of being governed by the circling of the moon
May terrify or irritate, but it's to nature's tune -
You're dancing to music we can't quite hear.

Prostate

Leaving through the waiting-room crowd
I re-hear his kind unhelpful words:
"Come to terms, I say to all my patients,
It's personal - everyone's experience
And values must differ. Some are aggrieved,
Some furious, some indignant, some relieved
(They often don't like to show that though!).
And you'll have your own reactions, I know".

But I don't know what mine are: can I make do
With memories no longer added to,
The stillness of dead photographs, the spoor
Of over forty years of each other?
And how can that match the fun of making more,
The eagerness, the thrust, and gasp, and judder?

Mr Cassandra

At sunrise we used to challenge them, shouting,
Clattering our shields, slagging off their women,
Sang our song at them, flashed at them, taunted them.
Lunch. Siesta. Then the fighting began,
Till truce was signalled by the evening *meltem*:
Everything as it should be and as we knew it was,
Ceremonious, reliable time!

Outside the war-zone, in the woods,
Slow-woofing pigeons and a wren's clear bellow:
In the fields under a copper sun
Women bringing water from the wells,
The barley harvest coming on,
Fat-bummed thunderclouds rising behind the hills:
We made love in the thickets: it all made sense.

In the town-centre with everyone looking
You first slumped inward, sighed,
Air driven out by the god's blow,
Suddenly incontinent, white-eyed,
When from your wet purple O
A child's voice uttered absurd, preposterous things:
We'd lose. A horse. Burning. Sacking. Downwards. Death
Of course I didn't believe you. No-one did.

"Who believes women anway?"
Said the others. "Bed?" I could hear them think.
"She tell you about that (nudge nudge) singer, eh?"
"Slap her about a bit." "Keep her off the drink."
"If it wasn't for who she is...."

How we laughed with relief when the doctor said
"No damage done. Stress you know. Something you ate?"
But it happened again. Whatever you cried
Could suddenly not be true. Until it was.
It was our future you had eaten,
So you were always weeping and resentful
And I was terrified, hoping never
To hear your child blab: "I'll love you forever."

Can you have been right all along?
Because now your horse has delivered its gangs,
You're lost somewhere out in the spark-torn night,
They're in our palaces, kicking the doors down,
And I'm about to believe you.

Couch Potato

Those were the days - he held the door, and brought
Surprises, giggled, called me when he woke,
My blood was supercharged, my body thought;
But once you're settled, it's just talk of work
And friends at work and watching boring sport,
Which lager's cheapest (why is it never his?).
You tell him fourteen times to walk the dog,
Forget your birthday - he already has -,
I actually have to ask him for a snog.
What have I done to turn him into this?
Before - a Prince, but afterwards - a frog.

Mr Black Beauty

She tried to hide me, not to see the signs -
Sweat, hard muscles, mucus clear or aphthous -
But I was there, snorting between the lines,
At stud between the chapters.

Mr Boadicea

Pull over to the kerb and stop under the elm-tree.
Back her round the corner, nice and slowly .....SLOW
...LEE,
Left hand down a bit, that's LEFT... Right, fine that time.
When you get down, just mind the off-side wheel-trim,
Don't want to cut our own leg off, now do we?

Why we need public transport

Three on Eurostar

The earth moves, just as you might expect,
Our speed and the mainly visual winds
Accelerate the slow clouds interchanges;
Two people opposite ...... Well, something has clicked:
Strangers at the start, they've now moved closer -
I frown at my novel and penetrate their minds.

They're talking in staccato bursts, finding
Ranges, setting up a database they're
Easy with; and clearly will move closer yet
From looks to trust and touch and understanding,
(Far-off villages, unknown crops wheel by)
Will the heavens too move for them somewhere?

But I, since I am now their maker, know:
He'll tire, wince at her passionate devotion -
She'll wither in his loss and drink too much -
He'll hate himself for it, nevertheless go -
She'll let herself be split and spurted into
By other loveless strangers to slow motion.

Whirling through fields of amaranth or sorghum
Of course my knowledge doesn't stop them.

Ferry

Against the afternoon sun and a grey horizon
Lies a sea like sandpaper.
A small girl, concentrating her gaze, is carrying two cups
of coffee back
        to her parents' table,
She glimpses the sandpaper and smiles.

The jealous coffee rebels
    it ruffles
    it prances
    it tittups
    it slurps itself
Noisily it breaks free and expands everywhere.
She weeps.

Stare, stare unflinchingly
To hold reality in shape.

16.09 Victoria to Brighton

The man opposite, reading Wilfred Thesiger's
Arabian Sands, has an articulated backbone.
Well, two actually - the second's a model,
Life-size, labelled, wrapped in clear plastic.
He holds it upright next to him, his arm protects it.
The fragment of skull droops shyly on his shoulder,
But below it's all there: discs, vertebrae,
(with coloured apophyses), sacrum, pubis....
As he reads, his hand warms the ischium.
I smile, but he's far away dreaming,
Of what, I wonder.

22

Early-morning bus

Between sleep and work makes for silence -
    the curly-headed driver
    two Chinese girls, eyes down, toes in
    the gang of schoolboys with uniform gelled spikes
    the fat man yawning in the aisle -
All are unresisting;
Their hearts, secret and open, wait
For love to strike.

Late-night bus

"nwanna si' there thin' we smell si' o' there do' they"
    "change for 50p then"
"aswa' I wa' go' say"
    "as' driver then"
"thin' we smell si' o' there"
    "ye' thass ri' then"
"aswa' I say"
    "sri' then"
"ye' sri'"

Going home from NightWriters,
Sandpapered by sonnets,
I meet old tensions:
Lush sonorities, dreams
Of hot shimmering summer,
Sunrise beyond tarns, caves of ice,
The beauty of anywhere I'm not;
    Or sordid pitiable this
And where would I be without it?

Taking off

The door slammed. We taxied slowly round.
Three children on the next seat chanted:
"Five. Four. Three. Two. One. Blast-off!"
We all laughed, so they chorused again:
"Five. Four. Three. Two. One. Blast-off!"
  and we went
   in a roar of engines, and up into the night,
   their mouths amazed
   at mastering the power of speech.

Bus stop

Every day we wait

why is it slow to come?

once or twice our looks meet
 if only....
the morning's silence fills our mouths

     shuffle   shuffle

why, why is it late?

     shuffle

Just when do we realise we've missed it?

Other Poems

Body-language

8 a.m. This is me going to work
A slept and nourished head
Brief-case, umbrella, notes (well-read),
A4, GNVQ, to speak
To other heads about abstractions -
Words, syntax, exam technique.

6 p.m. I turn. A peasant semi-crank,
I lobotomize furious brambles,
Deflower a bed, dismember trees,
Incinerate the amputated junk,
Lay concrete on the wreckage.
Dirty and exhausted, I get drunk.

I turn again. At every turn - revenge.

Reality's an inedible linguistic polyhedron

Everywhere people are writing poetry:
Gift-wrapping nouns, basting all the surfaces,
Jazzing-up edges with verbal upholstery,
Cosseting adjectives, adding a pinch
Of cinnamon, flounces, pralltriller, cornices:
Everywhere, reality's raw vertices -
Conjunctions, prepositions, - don't give an inch.

Guilty

What sequence led to this then?
Windows is threatening
"You have performed an illegal operation"

Have I aborted a print-job?
Down-loaded *"Daddy's little heart-throb"*?
Mis-spelled *Regina?* Unwittingly hacked
Into NATO's database? Peeped on an *act*?

It seeps in everywhere, a poison flame
That blackens, wearies, hides. Unspent,
The grey load is always more urgent,
Heavier. We pass it on in blame;
To lighten it, invent sin.

What have I left undone? What done?

Now it's 3 a.m. I'm going down to the police-station
To confess everything.

Again.

javelin

Whips out from behind,
Flies up, tail humming, stabs,
Suddenly, a heron.

Snow Poem

It's starting to snow as I speak
(A giant shakes his head; the world staggers)
Faster and faster flake blots out flake
Who can remember what was said last week?
A spinning sleet of hexagonal white
General and particular
Fat soggy clumps without a break
Swarm dizzily over the hedges.
    In no time
The lush seductive snow has tucked
Thisness, grime, knottiness out of sight;
    "Freeze!" I shout
And suddenly my lawn's a tablecloth
Breathless, captive, invulnerable,
A well-formed meta-artefact!

    Balance returns, and silence.

Sixty

I thought it would be a sleepy river,
But it's dizzying caracoles, swoops,
Flic-flacs, avalanches, triple toe-loops,
As kneecaps, memory, sense of smell,
Whole chunks of me vanish into never;
And something *is* at my door as well,
I no longer throw it open to greet
Registered letters, trick-or-treat,
But close it icily on canvassers,
Witnesses, double-glazers,
And the children leaving, my wife going out,
Goldengrove unleaving, certainty, doubt:
    Trapped in its jaws
    The blade of sunshine narrows.

Pique d'Endron

It was already late when I set out
(Anorak, hat, sun cream, glucose),
I strode up with a rush through the gardens
Where bees were bouncing a night-numbed rose
And frumping the dahlias about;
The tiny uproar of insects and martins
    Petering out

As I stepped on up to where the hills
Shrug off their clinging shawl of pines
Lushness and soil. Upwards there's no end
To the rise and rise of rockier skylines,
But the steady-falling beck reveals
The constant even pressure to descend
    That hugs my heels

Ever more clearly in the dull trudge
Zig zag zig zag across the slopes.
The mountain's shrinking to disappearance,
Scarcity is its new emblem, my hopes,
The sign of progress, At last the ridge
(A fly whines into the sudden distance)
    But still the peaks judge

Unfavourably. I plod above those
Blue, already sun-abandoned, combes,
Tackle the long slow slog to the height
Where up finishes for ever, and becomes
Past: *then* I've made it! Looking shows
A consummation of unhindered light,
    Mountains in rows,

Prim, unsuspected tarns. The muscular shot
Of achievement re-orders the whole world;
I sign the *Livre d'Or,* sprawl on the summit
Laughing, gulping my breath back, getting cold,
Wondering whether to stay or not.
Patient rocks in the last sunshine plummet,
    Distant doors shut

As that pure elated stab refuses
To be caught again. Now everywhere is down.
Will that be all then? Will I sink
To nothing? to potter in my dressing-gown,
To suck my teeth and peer through glasses,
To think whatever old men think
    When a girl passes.

Snowflakes

Words are snowflakes.
Weak, implacable, fruitless,
They drift into corners and crannies.
Smooth pillows of monochrome,
They soften harsh lines
    angles and moods;
Never, alas, the harsh owners -
Bark, stone, hearts.

Hand

I can cling and I can clench,
And squeeze, signal how many, press,
Slap, greet, wrench,
Two-finger a driver, soothe, bless.

Popping their seeds in the August sun
The nettles strut unbearably,
He wants them cleared, so I
Am wrapped, given a blade:
A perfect servant,
I turn the edge this way and that,
The swathes fall.

My mirror-twin and I can knead, placate,
Without us he's nothing; we strangle, pray,
Keep his rhythm, clear his plate,
Tirelessly we heal, applaud, weigh.

Eyes learn a lot too much,
And may take his side,
But ears are our patch,
Only we decide.

Mouth too can swerve: sing, kiss, say,
Only sometimes takes fright
To slobber, talk in the night, betray.
I'll soon put that right.

Old Peasant

Nailed to the grimy wall by the door,
Beside his hat and windproof jacket,
Was a photo of his grand-daughter,
A pudgy yearling. When he went to the barn
With pails of mash for the hens and rabbits,
To the copse with his long axe, or to the meadow
With scythe and sharpening-stone, he smiled back,
Made gurgling noises, planned how, when she came,
He'd teach her the old words, show her chicks hatching,
How they'd find names for the rabbits.

He died one winter. That spring his heirs
Took possession and the furniture,
Buried dead animals, threw away
Jacket, tools, a twenty-year-old photo.

Two Elephants

Somewhere between thunder and plod -
Amble, perhaps? but in any case
Patiently, momentously, heading
For the cool waters of the Niokolo
Across the motionless midday bush
Across our memories of dust
Their pachydermatous grey tons
Overawe the Renault 4L
Where we sit gripping hands.

From time to time they turn up like this
At their own deliberate pace;
We're growing old together,
Still pressing on towards unforgettable
Unattainable sweet waters.

Voices from the Cemetery

1

You can see for yourself names and dates

The records show other things:
  - It was that year's big wedding,
  - I succeeded his mother,
    Someone had to keep house after all.
  - Two sons stillborn, one on Christmas Day.
  - But two grew up, one's buried with us here,
    Epileptic, nevertheless Verdun.

Might memories and photos bring me to you?
  - When they brought the current
    I wouldn't have it in the house:
    What mightn't it get up to in the night,
    Creeping out to kill us?
  - In the only photograph you have,
    Slightly unfocused, I'm seventy,
    A dumpy peasant widow (headscarf,
    Apron, stick, mittens, tatty woolly)
    Smiling at my youngest with the camera.

Your efforts warm me, but it's not enough.
  - Was I happy? fulfilled? did I complain?
    What dreams, what tears, urged my boys on?
    Would I live it out over again?
    Am I glad to be gone?

2

We fell in love, sighed,
Were lost in each other's eyes;
Married, lived, died,
Now lost in each other's dust.

3

We shuffle forward:
Our turn to see the future
Clearer than the past.

4

"Not much of a life!" you exclaim,
"Born in June, dead before August ended"
But for me it's much the same
Laid rigid, silent, untended.

5

I wanted "Thank you for having me".
"Yes, yes, of course" they said.
But religion stole my voice instead
And what I got is what you see:
"Rest in Peace". Fat chance of that, then!

6

They bent the rules to put me here.

To you it looks a mess: but from inside?
Among strangers all my life? never happy?
No, it was right; not a failure of hope,
But a logical, ecstatic, suicide.

7

The entrance is just round the corner;
No seats - you either stand or lie.
So, respectful, silent, hoping not to cross
A real uninsulated mourner
Among the faceless piety
We wander round awkwardly
As if behind tinted windows
The dead defy our curiosity.

Fox

ditto marks on the road ahead?

no
what's left of a fox - flat reddish pelt
just the black ears pricked

as if he still trotted
under the glossy tar
delicately gulping field-mice
in former fields

So, what does it feel like?

First voice   "Yes, what it was like was this -
We had to run, run round the camp
Till we were dizzy and
Past that man him standing there now
And he pushed - pushed us on the shoulder
Yes on the arm here that's right
Really pushed. Many fell down
And just couldn't want to get back up
So they were - Oh you can't imagine
We didn't see them again
They were taken away, he did it."

Second voice   "You'll never know the hot flushes
Release from the long rosary of blood
That even so's an early death,
You're not a woman
You'll not live on diminished
You can't know what it's like."

Third voice   "Nor if you haven't been up to your eyes
In the black freezing sea -
I've watched a screaming child
Sucked from me, down the corridor, away…
You can't tell what it was like."

Me   No, I wasn't in that camp, or on that ferry
And I'll never be a woman
But can't you hear me?

Time's Rainbow at Montreal-de-Sos

Below the peaks, green is everywhere now.
But glaciers carved out this piton
that oversees five valleys and their trade -
and has for centuries.
Down the path come mules with baskets of waste.
Panting, we reach the top.

The girl running the dig explains
walls, mortar, dates, methods of restoration,
how, when, why. We try to imagine their lives.

Uncovering destroys,
you can only do it the once.
All anachronisms must be noted,
dust sieved and sorted, saved
for subtler technologies than ours.

Swifts flicker jaggedly by
mountains I'll never climb again.

It's a rainbow:
        from hue
            to hue
                we
                    slip

                    endlessly.

Symbols in the Graveyard

I'm clearing nettles from a family tomb.
I brush soil and dead twigs from the slab,
De-moss the headstone to give survival-room
For names at least. Then I assault time to come:
I rip up roots, snip iris-leaves, clip
Back an immortality bursting up in
Slow-slithering root and raw fountains of green.

Why all this paraphernalia of tombs?
As a young man I used to mock
Appalling verses, plastic chrysanthemums,
Scrunchies of wild olive! Bleached photos of old frumps!
Comfort-blankets for the comfortless dead!
Now only the metaphysical will suit -
Don't want to end as doggerel or a root.

Am I preparing it for me? or me for it?
Every few minutes I have to pause, redress
My ageing back, catch my lost breath, mop sweat,
And glare at the surrounding hills; then target
Litter - no condoms this year, thank goodness;
As flesh nags both more and less, that voice
Of its dominion increasingly annoys.

Right at the foot I find a moulted snakeskin,
A tough transparent brown, present in every way
Even the eye-scales; just put aside, outgrown,
Shuffled off here in the quiet sun.
Renewal; continuation; I think today.
How warm and private for such an intimate act,
I would have thought, once, matter-of-fact.

Summer

Summer's kazoo,
Humming sibilants, voiced fricatives,
The bee-filled air

In Banjul Cemetery

i.m. F.R.Mensah

No, he doesn't know (mint from my hotel room
I asked the watchman). So through my bifocals
I read each stone - getting to know the locals!
What they cover is much as it is back home,
The merely physical: bones, poor tattered rind;
I quarter the hot dunes where they lie confined.
A white wind, stiff as paint, catches my breath
But I can stroll on with a quiet mind,
Flaunting potential, the future's star recruit,
I'm nosy, patronising, resolute -
    How different from this death!

No, this just won't do; after an hour
I'm sweating, bitten, fed-up. Why can't they trim
The plots, rule lines, signpost and number them,
Put them in alphabetical order?
Suddenly I'm one of nature's SS -
To straighten up the ranks and fill the spaces
I send them all to death; with my blackshirts
I swagger, I parade, I attack their mess -
This dump is where they were always bound
Salt, dry marram grass, dry unresisting ground -
    Just déserts: just desérts.

No, they aren't all innocents at all of course
Brought here by massacre, but casual dead,
By weakness, accident, a kinked thread
Of genes, mistakes, a wrong or unmade choice.
Complacently, I sum up their abstractions -
Names, dates, verses, prayers, appreciations -
Physical now is me, we've nothing in common
But only till I must match their imperfections;
Bald, slackening, an albino stranger,
Why should I survive a minute longer?
    I slink guiltily on.

No, I didn't find it. To do what I'd come for,
I chose a place at random looking out to sea,
To make it real this time and not more me
Again, to clear my mind of spite and anger,
Contempt and irony; hoping, praying,
That short black good-humoured angels singing
Hymns will throng the startled air to raise these dead
With harps and hallelujahs heralding
God "who wipes away all tears from their eyes,
And there shall be no more death." Do I believe this?
No ...
        Maybe.....
            But you did.

Overnight Snow

Tentative and crunchy
Traffic on the morning snow;
Behind thick curtains
I lie in warm denial.

Like It

The message that comes back is this:
"Suddenly, just like that, it stops,
You'll never want to do it again;
An end to being shackled to a lunatic,
To being forced to ride a mustang.
Accept and be thankful." Yes, I can see ....
But surely somewhere there's a plus -
Some habits, trains of feeling, images,
A lesson learned? You mean ....

Like a growing girl?
Appalled to find how much more closely
The innocent movements of her childish body
Now fit this nubile one, the flesh
Partners the ripening mind.

Like a stranger in the street?
Who comes slowly through my lens,
The humours, rods and cones, black screen,
Shedding something at every step
So entering my mind naked
Rippling urgently, surprising
Me as much as it would her
If she, looking deep into my eyes,
Could see this X-film starring her --
And I in hers? I look away quickly.

Like all the pain and anger
In unconsummated marriages,
Desires invented, body-lying,
Teenage prurience-and-prudery,
Dilation-and-curettages,

Guilt-driven rows, sterility.
Like those who give themselves to quantity?
Who learn a predatory competence;
Tigers sure of their superiority
In having so much more of what all want
(Though missing the point rather), they've a sense
Of other lives that breeds contempt. And loss.

Like why I no longer dream of you?
Your double, that perfect-breasted succubus,
You-but-not-you, has gone for ever.
Now that you're one, even asleep I know
It's you there, faintly snoring, decorous -
To dream would be to prefer.

So apres-sex is going to be like this then:
Love with its necessary tingle,
Corrupt, dangerous, irresponsible,
Has changed for good; and you can like it.

Walking Past Heifers

What on earth am I up to
Walking past their fence?
Am I a danger? a portent?
Why am I alone? where are my sibs, my tribe?
Free to go where I want, why do I want?
Why don't I stay put,
Farting in flagrant splendour,
Fertilising tomorrow's cud?

White-eyed with amazement, they galumph
Lumpishly alongside. I stop;
They huddle round, jostle,
One snorts, one clambers on a back;
All yearn to put their questions,
If I had time; if speech would only come.

Tribe

There is a tribe somewhere
Dogon? Mapuche? Kamchadal?
Who are travelling backwards -
Backwards through time, that is,
Facing what they see clearest:
The familiar, exploitable past.
The future lies in wait behind their babies,
Looms unpredictably at every back,
"Look behind you!" they cry;
It pours round them into colour and light.

On long trips to traditional hunting-grounds
Through sahel or mulga, across the silent plains,
Only by trotting blindly on
Can they understand fresh spoor.

Home again that evening, round the fire,
With wife and kids - they playing cat's cradle,
She greasing another hide perhaps -
They remember the journey:
"Today," they joke,
"my feet have been on back-to-front".

But bed-time stories keep off the darkness
With their traditional comfort:
"And they all lived happily ever after".

Cello

A river under the irises
The cello talking to itself

Sahara

I welcome all who come.

Everything's laid out:
    luxuries of light
    manna and hidden water-holes
    a pathless freedom

What can they make of barkhans, fennecs?
Such pleasure to match their ingenuities with mine!

Ah! I smother my darlings
With skies of black velvet;
My rich maternal moon
Shows them their bones
        their needlessness
        themselves

Why don't more come?

Double Edge

Walking behind a woman in the night,
Up side-streets, on well-lit avenues,
On the short-cut past the building site,
Cross the road, chink change, scuff your shoes:
Look! No balaclava, no two-foot knife.

There is no answer to her fear,
Resent it all you like, you'll bear
This blade, this necessary guilt.

St. Catherine's Lock

I could cross of course and reach cow-bitten fields
Scorned by towpath-walkers and picnickers in punts,
        I was enough;
The dusty water where the sunlight turned cartwheels
Charged over the weir; house-martins skittered; once
I caught a perch, but mainly sat there *in* and *of*
        A natural sum.
        If I go back, I want it to be
        As changed as I am:
        Perfect only in my memory.

Sahara 2

Look empty, do I?
Autoclaved? Monotonous?
A breathless, uninspiring waste?

You simply aren't trying hard enough:
Every one of my opaque hissing granules,
Shaded, twinkling, burred, is different -
Don't talk to me of snowflakes -
And in between are gaps as various,
Where lurk my seeds.

Once every twenty years they open
To marram, acacia, thorn.
But I, among blown plumes of dust
In these eternal spaces,
This surfeit of variety,
I don't change or compromise,
I'm all the things you're never going to know.

Poem for Reading Silently

"A rose is a rose is a rose"

Sorry, could we take that again?
Surely "a rose" only seems a rose,
It is "a rose".
And as it imitates a rose,
" a rose" is imitated by "" a rose"".
So a rose "is" "a rose" ""is"" ""a rose""
Is that it?

Tender petal a verbal construct?
Warm scent a stock reaction?
Curled fleshy pink an imperfect incarnation?

It's a metaphysical tease,
A linguistic labyrinth.

And yet it's there.

Spring

I'm watching an X-film: out there
my garden seethes with lust,
squirrels, blackbirds, next-door's cats -
            all at it.
on the roof, pigeons coo and screw,
crocuses and daffodils exert
flamboyant reproductive organs.

            Ah, nature!

This mocking gets me even:
no animal can do that.

Over Dinner

My daughter and her husband
Are coming to dinner.
After sherry and nibbles, there'll be
Roast duck with turnips,
A decent claret,
Civilised conversation and laughter;
Coffee with an early-landed cognac.
Familiar codes and references line
The short-cuts of love.

It wasn't always so;
Down in the aromatic swirls I see:

- a five-year-old, who lives in the looks of others,
  dancing on a Spanish beach at sunset

- at puberty her hair and she
  fizz up in tight snarls

- fifteen - her eyes are blank as galaxies
  the nest opens a mouth, its cuckoo speaks

- later she steals ashtrays from every joint
  God alone knows what she smokes

- 4 a.m., whose voices?
  a car-door slams, tyres squeal,
  I listen for her key

And now? "And now you can be friends!"
Announce the books,
Cosily, triumphantly;
But "friends" is no good,
"Friends" can't be what we want,
Some scars worth hiding must remain.

Waste

Sculptor or wood-carver, pondering oak or stone,
Can see the mother-and-child, the patient shapes,
The grain waiting to be hair or pleated drapes.
Workers of metal, sugar, garden, onyx, bone,
Know what must be removed from where you start,
And what's left over, you can reconstitute
As compost, or eat, or melt down, or burn.

Words tempt further: they fuse, repel, preclude,
Though each has its integrity: what you take
Is what's taken from, there's no figure, no strake;
You can't solder, or recast, or substitute.
And yet there's waste here too - clumsy, opaque,
Strange in the mouth: dross, clinker, swarf, lees,
Scissel, noil, fenks - what's to be done with these?

Power

Gardeners, who force their will on lawns and borders,
Dog-trainers (why don't they tackle a cat?),
Road-ragers who've lost it, compulsive hoarders
Mad to keep their grip on time, wielders of fat,
People who keep you waiting, applauders
Compelling an encore, preachers, your M.P.,
Rapists, gun-freaks, carriers-out of orders,
And then there's masochists and the military ....

But me? No, no thanks; force, impose, command,
None of them's me; I just want to let you call,
Open doors, invite you in to look around,
Diverting you with images and rhyme as
I seep into your mind like Alzheimer's,
To get you where I want you, after all.

47

Grandfather

I ask what it used to be like
He's kept it all, thrown nothing away

      a wrought-iron hinge, an inkwell
      cloth-covered black-and-white flex,
      strips of leather, a nappy-pin,
      some 8 x 1¼" woodscrews,
      beeswax, a magnet, washers ....

"May come in useful. You never know."

now his fingers drag,
A heavy rattle,
Through the speech in his scrap-box.
He picks,
Carefully,
To improvise what needs to be said..

Snaps

That's my grandmother, second from the right,
Just behind Dad. How happy she looks!
It's not how I remember her: glum mouth tight
As a sprung trap, her black flounced frocks
Turgid with disapproval.
              But somebody can have loved her.

Now here's a famous one - do you remember
That drive to the coast in '70 was it?
You're wrapped up and say it was November.
If I've told you once .... I can still feel the heat,
Summer sun on the shingle,
              You *know* you've got it wrong, dear.

Ah, not that one, who's kept this, of me making
A real fool of myself with Pat? Luckily
There's none of worse embarrassments: faking
Emotions, cowardice, greed, treachery,
And if only that was all!
                    What can be made of such silt?

Some I don't understand - just run them through
Now and then, to wonder what, and if, they mean:
Six ruffians seen through an open window
Playing cards at night at a small French station
Where there was a water-mill.
                    Why this, of all I've felt?

Who's this in bunches, holding my hand? Or this -
Thin, head back, laughing - nobody I know.
But definitely in our garden, *Chris
Bellamy* someone's pencilled on the back. No!
It's just not possible,
                    I know it can't be him.

Liar! Cheat! One of my worst enemies
At school. What could he be doing at my home?
Can we have made up? No, because I always
See him as someone to be different from,
A negative example.
                    Is either of these pictures true?

The hard thing is to admit the error:
It isn't sepia or black-and-white
That shape our lives, or even *Trucolor,*
But this blurred transfer, like a parasite,
Random and unanswerable
                    Whatever uses we put it to.

Forest Floor

I scuff up woodland leaves
    dances in the shafts of light
    mineral cosmic dust
    mites   spores
    old pollen
    unspoken words
    shards of elytra
    packets of spider sperm
    dry scalings of acorns

        passion's debris
        a mind's floor

Give and Take

Drizzle, depression, misgivings and mud.
Under the middle toe of my right foot
Has lost all feeling. I kneaded it
Absent-mindedly this morning. Ignored,
It closes in for the kill: a verruca?
Gangrene? necrosing fasciitis? dry rot?
Do I remove my shoe, face a dead-white spot,
Leprosy caught on a trip to Africa?

I hunch into my hood, stalk on along
The dripping hedgerows, tinkle my bell. Peasants
Flee, or snatching up children and flints,
They loose their dogs. Desperately I prong
These off with my stick; then surface. Real mutts
Are growling, leaping at me. And no wonder!
But I prong them off too, happily: it's
Always good to be reminded that giver
And taker must coincide, and differ.

High Summer

Hills stretch out in languor
Less noise than pear-blossom
Falling in the night

Fears

She walks down the street under an empty sky

Suddenly it's swirling with giant spiders
- alert still eyes, staccato hysterical legs -
They chitter, bat-like. In a rising wind
a forest's twanging drowns all other sound.
Everywhere, his looks guess her everywhere.
Sea-surges smelling of fish and flowers
Pluck at her thighs. Overhead
Crackling drapes of aurora
Design her an icy future
Where pallid flames make darkness visible.
Diagonals zig-zag. The moon unhoods
Herself. Heavy blood whirrs in his temples.

A robin sings. She walks on under an empty sky.

Plagiarist

Playwrights make plays,
Wheelwrights make wheels,
I can't do better than copy right.

Reversible Images

1

Sometimes the clicker jams:

a girl…..
a girl…..
a girl…..
But suddenly
                    Click!   An old woman
Click!   A pretty girl
                    Click!   A shrivelled crone.
A candlestick becomes
                    a face-to-face becomes
a candlestick
                    a face-to-face…..

All these depend on me
Doors, locks, fences, wrong or right,
Right or left, black or white,
A ship alone at sea.

2

Sex would be another such,
A slimy penetration
Of something we'd rather not
Know detail of -
                    a tender
Sparkling darkness
As near to love as possible
                    as far from, too.

3

It's not an Ishihara test (some can, some can't)
Come on, you can make it:
Outside, spring's cherry blancmanges
Are coming apart in the rain
Snowing the drive with unseasonal dandruff.
     Or: it's dark on a misty field
     In winter, those ragged trees
     Are terrifying bandages -
     You put the eyeholes in.

Some days are different though:
You dig potatoes - it's not a treasure hunt
(This year's dark cream, odd ones from last year red)
Or fishing. No, it's just digging potatoes.
     Maybe you light a bonfire:
     With a slow bang all the stuff goes up,
     The column of heat punches a hole in the dark
     You shield your eyes from the reality;
     Click.

Ageing

It's so half-hearted;
My strongest emotion
A weak irritation,
My sole ambition
To sit, like a lizard,
In the slow sun,
Blinking.

Eccentricity

Are poets odd? All these chaps one averts
One's mind from - reeling by supermarket doors,
Resting their socks on train seats, counting cars,
Bellowing at fuchsias - can they be poets?

Or those one hears of, who fly on opiate,
See angels, invade Dalmatia, or rob graves,
Take lobsters for walkies, traffic in slaves
To affirm their quiddity, write about it?

To be a poet should I put myself through
"A long, thought-out, disordering of the senses"?
Seek out "more meaningful" experiences?
Try my hardest to be unlike you?

But what I'm passionate about is near:
Autumn, love, parents, being in a hurry:
It's not just messages from the periphery
There's more than plenty to be said right here.

So I brown the meat and onions, peel the spuds,
Season, stir, cover. In just half an hour
It's ready to eat. Later there's pans to scour
And dirty plates to slip into the suds
Softly. In ordinariness is power.

Space Music

The rings of Saturn
A galaxy's compact disc
Music of the spheres

Mind

That like a root (only the tip absorbs)
    must be forever thirsting out;
    it chases off on doggy errands,
    stabs like a park-keeper.

It crosses deserts at full throttle
    inserts itself between the molecules
    of limestone, cannel, gneiss;
    rides tsunamis, barging through tons.

It idles in a clear current
    dawdling its fins, then
    darts in fright
    a curl of sand is lazily carried away.

Flame-like it flickers back and forth
    - a boy swiping the hedgerows
    - bones sharpen through the skin
    - it pounces on logarithms.

It's a captive bolt, that, sated,
    bloodied, returns again and again
    to the reliable flesh on the sofa,
    where it can become what it is:

Void. Darkness moves upon it;
    ideas in search of form
    and substance creep in.
    It secretes me a pearl.

Rotation of Crops

A G & T at 30 000 ft?
"Mineral water, no ice, for me, please."
I tilt my seat and think of you. The in-flight
Magazine offers a map, malts, 'fragrances'.
My neighbours have ' a place out there.' In here, at
Cocoon cloud nine, we're cramped, belted, sat.

But I'm dreaming of under warm brown soil,
Floury/waxy; second earlies/maincrop;
Reds/whites; Ulster Chieftain/Pink Fir Apple;
And the slow toil - trenching, earthing-up;
Feet in thick murk, I lift and clamp and fight
Scab, potato cyst eelworm, slugs, wart, blight.

But I'm dreaming of asepsis, monotone;
A high, clear, flute-like, impersonal womb,
Where, abstract, irresponsible, waited-on,
Along a great circle or a loxodrome,
I travel to identical places whose
Identical palaces offer identical views.

But I'm dreaming of varieties -
The willing tracklessness that love goes through,
Its freedoms and subserviences -
Dominant, Incomparable, Tender and True ....

March Twigs

Firm winds massage them
Knowingly - out at the tips
Explodes the summer

SOCO

rips up the tape
the carpet surrenders old hair;
dust, grit and corpuscles
come out of hiding,
dead skin and fibres
tell my secret past:
    here I trod
      there put the bag down
      in that chair told a lie;
seems innocent enough,
what have I done?
but it's all there
it's all life's evidence
for the prosecution.

Clocks

Clonk! Oh the excitement - seven, up and alone,
I read in the kitchen, breathless; clink!
My grand-parents' clock dished out its two-tone
Ticks. Couldn't they see, didn't they think
It was too like a dead march, a count-down?
Why didn't they change it for a silent one?

But now a grandfather myself, up early
From insomnia, not for the breathless fun,
Fighting the fuzziness of seventy,
I sit with a book in my own kitchen;
The clock's still there, but now I read furiously,
Each word survival, each tick a victory.

Communing with Nature

Now it's a worn spray of grass between the flags.
South African marigolds. On the daisyless lawn
Fat tabbies lumber after birds.
A fox looks at me behind the double-glazing.

It was already nearly too late
When sceptical Richard Johnson would have looked
In Januarie 1556,
In the North-East Passage, by the Kara Sea.
Five reindeer offered themselves,
Were welcomed, gralloched, boiled; became
Hot suet, greasy juice and hair, burnt muscle,
A smoking bundle of marrow-bones.

Then in the tent the Priest arose,
A veil of fish-ribs, seal- and glutton-teeth
Covered his bodily eyes. Drumming and hallooing
"So manie times he becommeth as it were madde"
Ran a scalded sword through his full belly
("I layde my finger on the poynt behinde.")
Two men gripped the ends of a noose
As the deerskin slip-knot lopped off
His head and arm into the seething pot.
I tried to rise, but they held me down,
All "singing & out calling Oghaoo!
Oghaoo! Oghaoo! " for hours.

Beast came through the dead man's shirt
Leaving no trace.

And presently the Priest,
Siberian shaman, angekkok,
Re-acquainted with death and our deeper selves,
One with our deer, with the foxes, the wolverines,
Lifted up his reborn head, came forth to the fire
In silence, and told us what we had to do.

But it was already too late.

And now milk comes from bottles, carrots from Kenya,
Meat from wrapped trays of polystyrene,
Understanding from books.
We see nothing ripped up, nothing robbed from calves,
The rending flesh, the bone slowly cracked:
Only far constellations tell us what we are,
No totem offers its throat.

Port Selda

No birds were singing in any shire:
The harbour swirled with quarrelling gulls;
A grey downpour hissed on the waves
That crashed against the crumbling walls.

I wanted to be anywhere else,
With you; all I saw was a town
No whit less ruinous and still
Than the high gantries rusting down.

All afternoon on the bare platform
Shadows grew damper and colder.
The train was late. Of course it was.
Oh yes, I remember Port Selda.

Excavating a Midden

I've been allotted a section. Under the scanty turf
Nearly all of it's oyster-shells, heavy, calcareous,
Like splintered, organic, stone. Some were made into scrapers,
But most were simply chucked over their shoulders as they sat
Kippered, pelted, barefoot, slurping oysters from dawn to dusk.

The slow anonymous shells have earned the right to be patient,
They're going further than us; we zip across their horizons
Like soft comets. Centuries have piled them dizzily deep.
Head down over my trench, I brush out more fleeting remains:
Dry interstitial soil, intrusive debris, roots,
Uncover fish vertebrae, a shoulder-blade, a tibia.

Which way are we moving through time? the midden's bottom
Is its oldest memories; but skin that wrinkles and flakes,
Sparse hair, whirling head, slow joints - my oldest's to come.
Leaning to my beginnings, fermented, composted,
I blossom forwards, sink away into my depths.

Cardinal Points

Going South, we fall on strange tongues
That stick to the palate. We lall
Fang, Telugu, Tagalog, Chol.
Darkness comes to the pounding of pestles
And a blue drift of wood-smoke.
Under its wing we scatter to compounds
For mealies or foufou.
The drums and the dancing begin;
Warm rhythms invade our ears,
Our blood accelerates.

All's water Westwards, and its moody surges:
Waves clap and roar;
Tsunamis range the wide horizons.
Sunrise and sunset,
Orange and ultramarine,
Measure out the world.
Nobody's ever felt like this before.
Elvers, the Sargasso Sea, the Doldrums,
Hy Brasil, the Islands of the Blest,
Here we come!

We can follow Marco Polo to the East
Past shrivelling lakes.
Rivers slacken to sand.
An ageing grit clogs the streets
Of Bokhara, Khiva, Balkh.
By white-washed farms,
Where apricots balloon tinily,
A frosty wind nibbles the trellised grapes.
Who are these masked women? Where is the sea?

Travelling north, we meet Blackfaces,
Herdwicks and Ayrshires.
Landscapes are cleaner,
There's none of that scrubby straggle
Of bramble and sycamore,
Though hanks of wool flap on gate-bars.
Dry walls restrict these fields. Stone rules.
And its objectiveness enters us
Bit by bit as we approach
The one unrehearsable stop.

Grandfather's Gaze

Across the hot, over-furnished flat,
The family's visiting chit-chat,
His urgent gaze weighed on my childhood,
A message? a challenge? surely not a plea?
So far beyond anything I understood
That for years I carried it with me,
In airports, sleep, exams; at conferences,
Or on a mountain-top, or fishing, say,
I took it out, bluish, opaque, watery,
Remade the effort he still insisted on.
Now, slowly, I've given up those silences,
That wordless worrying at what I've found
I'll never be able to live up to;
It's become my loss too.

Trails

With slow-piped icing on the blue
(and unlike meek-tailed comets)
high planes are trailing their past
today
                out
                        endlessly
tethered to what's invisible
just like you or me by our days

and which of us can tell
what may be rippling along that scent
surging after us
tracking us down
what shark or angel?

Whale-watching off the Azores

We're no longer alone:
We're crossing a motorway
In sea-mist, on a sleek swell,
Engine and Portuguese stop,
Open-mouthed the sailors listen
About to remember something -

There, only yards away, a black berg

        up ....
Rolls   over ....
               long ....
                    longer...
And more everywhere as big as museums
Echo the first, shapeless as swollen lights,
Huge hushing snorting pops -
Temporary islands are breathing all around.

Next to the boat
A calf the size of your bedroom slides over,
Blows oily, fishy, salty
Memories of our water-logged womb -
Can we be friends?

A tail rises, a clutch of barnacles on the left fluke,
They're going down, one after the other.
Blank sea-sheep, just warm fish,
These meteors of blubber plunge out of our lives,
Return us to the mist
Now sprayed with a fading stink.

In the present, though laughing and cheering,
We're on our own.

Some ways of coping with passion

1

In the suburbs at night, rose scent
Stalks the unwary passer-by;
Nightingales in every shrubbery
Sing to their aching throats' content;
White moonlight blackens the olive-trees,
Dims the lamps patient endeavour.
To set one's passions above these!
A leaf to every wind that blows,
To be seventeen for ever!

2

He   I took her out at first because
           Most of my friends used to treat
           Sex all as a matter of course,
           And talk about it in the street;
           And I wasn't one to be left out,
           So when I met her at a dance
           I asked her out and quickly got
           What I wanted; that's how she caught
           Me, though I don't regret the chance.

She   I married him for the money;
           Well, not the money itself
           Exactly, but money gives me
           A feeling of protecting myself
           In case of anything happening.
           He's got a steady job and won't
           Leave me short; we both like gardening
           Touring, cuddling and ballroom-dancing:
           What better husband could I want?

Both	Now look here, you just leave us alone,
	We aren't interfering with you
	Are we? We were alright on our own
	Before you came telling us how
	People in other places you knew
	Went mad after their wives
	Had died, or changed their whole lives
	Just at their sweetheart's nod -
	Quite different from us, thank God!

3

This is midsummer alright,
Rather hazy and indefinite.
Even the yellowhammers doze
Sunk in intense repose.
Over the intolerant afternoon
Heat-bigoted June
Struts on the year's meridian,
Its own emotionless criterion.
All time shrivels to now
This barren artificial fire
Burns out all colour and diversity -
Indifference, desire, orange, blue,
Are sterile momentary ash
Smashed into conformity.

Autumn is preferable, a joint compromise,
Both June and December,
In whose equinoctial poise
The minutes bring order
To the moment's chaos;
Emotions gradually disentangle,
What birds there are can all be heard,
Mists even are definable
And the dry blackthorns covered
With lush berries. Ambivalent time!
All of whose gifts are fruit,
And let reality,
Though swadddled in their bland windings,
Still, incontrovertible and scalene, cut.

Night-Ride and Sunrise

Unpatterned simple black
Outside this one-dimensional zoom;
More in my mind than in my eyes
Buildings, woods, hedges, marginally loom;
Easy to know where everyone is,
    Which way to take.

Day moves in overhead
A pale crack unkeys the dark arches,
Variety splurges, green and white,
Dutch barns, spinneys, elms; on the verges
A scattering of rabbits comes to light,
    Some of them dead

Unignorably show
Where night's murderous dazzles have passed;
I can hear a wren sing; sunlight blares out,
All vegetation begins its breakfast;
Everywhere beckons, warm, infinite,
    Beguiling, so

I stop. Pretend it's to pee
Or stretch and yawn, or tread the quiet turf,
But note how much easier it is
To fly in a regardless curve
As arrows do, than to face choices -
    Which is being free.

This way? That? The rich weight
Of all possible courses holds us back;
Only they *will* fizzle out, night *will* be
Coming, when, squeezed neatly in the dark
Rectangular box, we all, easy or free,
    Resume our flight.

Poem Acknowledgements
These poems have appeared in the following magazines:

The Affectionate Punch	Mr Beeton
Anon	Cardinal Points
Candelabrum	Moving on; Forest Floor
Envoi	Old Peasant; Mr Scheherazade; Body language; Whale watching off the Azores; St Catherine's Lock; Give and Take; Mind; Reality's an Inedible Linguistic Polyhedron; Trails; Communing with Nature
The Interpreter's House	Eccentricity
Iota	Mr Sleeping Beauty; Waste ; Grandfather ; Infidelities; Power; 16.09 Victoria to Brighton; Double Edge
The New Writer	Mr Cinderella; Mr Black Beauty; Mr Cassandra; Mr Boadicea
Obsessed with Pipework	Sock; Sahara
Orbis	The Man who Married a Spinster; Mr Mona Lisa; Snowflakes
Pennine Platform	Eve; Mr Olympia; Excavating a Midden Reversible Images; Prostate; Three on Eurostar; 60; Some Ways of Coping with Passion
Poetry Monthly	Early-morning Bus; Guilty; Two Elephants
Poetry Nottingham International	We Grew Colder; March Twigs; Ferry; Spring
Rialto	Clocks
Seam	Taking off
South	Snow Poem
South by South-east	javelin
Staple	Mr Griselda; Going to Bed; Fox; So, what does it feel like?; Symbols in the Graveyard; Like it
still	In Bed; Cello

Lightning Source UK Ltd.
Milton Keynes UK
UKHW01f1704260618
324819UK00006B/265/P